U.S. Department of Justice
Federal Bureau of Investigation
Criminal Justice Information Services Division

I0413679

Crime in Schools and Colleges:

A Study of Offenders and Arrestees Reported via National Incident-Based Reporting System Data

James H. Noonan and Malissa C. Vavra
Crime Analysis, Research and Development Unit
Criminal Justice Information Services Division
Federal Bureau of Investigation
October 2007

Introduction

Schools and colleges are valued institutions that help build upon the Nation's foundations and serve as an arena where the growth and stability of future generations begin. Crime in schools and colleges is therefore one of the most troublesome social problems in the Nation today. Not only does it affect those involved in the criminal incident, but it also hinders societal growth and stability. In that light, it is vital to understand the characteristics surrounding crime in schools, colleges, and universities and the offenders who reportedly commit these offenses so that law enforcement, policy makers, school administrators, and the public can properly combat and reduce the amount of crime occurring at these institutions.

Tremendous resources have been used to develop a myriad of federal and nonfederal studies that focus on identifying the characteristics surrounding violent crime, property crime, and/or crimes against society in schools. The objective of such studies is to identify and measure the crime problem facing the Nation's more than 90,000 schools and the nearly 50 million students in attendance.[1] The findings of these studies have generated significant debates surrounding the actual levels of violent and nonviolent crimes and the need for preventative policies. Some research indicates there has been an increase in school violence activities, such as a study from the School Violence Resource Center which showed that the percentage of high school students who were threatened or injured with a weapon increased from 1993 to 2001.[2] Other research notes decreases in student victimization rates for both violent and nonviolent crimes during a similar time period (1992–2002).[3] Moreover, the circumstances surrounding crime in schools, colleges, and universities are not always the ones that gain wide notoriety. The most significant problems in schools are not necessarily issues popularly considered important as most conflicts are related to everyday school interactions.[4] Furthermore, the National Center for Education Statistics notes that "it is difficult to gauge the scope of crime and violence in schools without collecting data, given the large amount of attention devoted to isolated incidents of extreme

---

[1] National Center for Education Statistics, "Public Elementary and Secondary Students, Staff, Schools, and School Districts: School Year 2002-03 E.D. TAB," NCES 2005-314, US Department of Education, 2005.

[2] School Violence Resource Center, "Weapons and Schools II Fact Sheet," University of Arkansas System, June 2003.

[3] National Center for Education Statistics, "Indicators of School Crime and Safety: 2004," US Department of Education, 2004.

[4] National Institute of Justice, "Crime in the Schools: A Problem-Solving Approach" (Summary of a Presentation by Dennis Kenney, Police Executive Research Forum), August 1998.

school violence."[5] These conflicting conclusions concerning the ability to measure the overall situation of crime in school, college, and university environments make it difficult for policy makers to assess the effectiveness of policies and their impact on this phenomenon.

The Nation's need to understand crime as it occurs at schools, colleges, and universities was officially placed into law by the US Congress with the passage of the Jeanne Clery Disclosure of Campus Security Policy and Campus Crime Statistics Act[6] (Clery Act). Prompted by the 1986 rape and murder of a 19-year-old Lehigh College student in her dorm room, the Clery Act requires universities and colleges to report crime statistics, based on Uniform Crime Reporting (UCR) definitions, to the Department of Education (ED) and to disclose crime statistics to nearly 16 million students attending any one of the Nation's approximately 4,200 degree-granting, post-secondary institutions.[7] The Clery Act, most recently amended in 2000, demands stiff financial penalties from post-secondary institutions found to misreport crime statistics to the ED. Such penalties are currently set at $27,500 per incident.[8] Though the Clery Act requires colleges and universities to report their crime data to the ED, neither it nor any other Federal legislation requires these institutions to report the data to the UCR Program.

Situations surrounding crime at school locations vary based on the offender's motive and the intended victim. For example, incidents involving student offenders and student victims constitute the stereotypical definition of crime at schools, colleges, and universities where the offender and victim are present to participate in the activities occurring at the institution. However, there are situations involving adult and/or juvenile offenders and victims, where the school serves only as an offense location because neither the offender nor the victim is present to participate in school functions. Criminal acts due to political motivation, hate crimes, and crimes perpetrated by offenders against victims who are not instructors or students and have no other relation to the school are examples of such situations.

In an attempt to shed light on crime in schools, colleges, and universities, this study used incident-based crime data the FBI received from a limited set of law enforcement agencies through the UCR Program. Some of the findings are perhaps contrary to popular perceptions; for example, over the 5-year study period, the use of knives/cutting instruments was over three times more prevalent than the use of a gun. (Based on Table 8.) Other findings reflect conventional wisdom; for example, males were nearly 3.6 times more likely to be arrested for crime in schools and colleges than females. (Based on Table 12.)

Objective

Data from a variety of sources about crime in schools and colleges and characteristics of the people who commit these offenses provide key input in developing theories and operational applications that can help combat crime in our Nation's schools, colleges, and universities. Given the myriad of data available, the objective of this study is to particularly analyze data submitted to the FBI's UCR Program by law enforcement agencies. It examines specific characteristics of offenders and arrestees who participated in criminal incidents at schools and colleges from 2000 through 2004. Because the study dataset is not nationally representative, readers should be cautious in attempting to generalize the findings. (See the Methodology section for data caveats.)

---

[5] National Center for Education Statistics, "Indicators of School Crime and Safety: 2005," NCJ 210697, November 2005.

[6] H.R. 3344, S.1925, S.1930.

[7] National Center for Education Statistics, "Digest of Education Statistics 2003," NCES 2005-025, US Department of Education, December 2004. (Numbers are for the 2001-02 school year.)

[8] Security On Campus, Inc. "Clery Act History," *n.d.* <http://www.securityoncampus.org/schools/cleryact/cleryact.html>, accessed on 08/03/2007.

Data

The data used for this study reside in databases maintained by the UCR Program, which the FBI manages according to a June 11, 1930, congressional mandate. Law enforcement agencies nationwide may choose to participate in the UCR Program by voluntarily submitting crime data in one of two formats: the Summary Reporting System or the National Incident-Based Reporting System (NIBRS). Not all UCR data, however, reflect sufficient detail to be useful for this study. Therefore, only the UCR data gathered via the NIBRS were used.

Methodology

The NIBRS was designed in the 1980s to enhance the Summary Reporting System by capturing detailed information at the incident level. Once the system was developed, the FBI began collecting NIBRS data in 1991 from a small group of law enforcement agencies. By the end of 2004, approximately 33 percent of the Nation's state and local law enforcement agencies covering 22 percent of the US population reported UCR data to the FBI in the NIBRS format. (See Table 1.) In addition, the percentage of crime reported to the UCR Program via the NIBRS had risen from 13 percent in 2000 to 20 percent in 2004. However, increases in the amount of crime reported via NIBRS do not necessarily indicate increases in crime in general or the actual occurrences of crime in schools. Increases in the number of NIBRS offenses may be largely the result of more law enforcement agencies using the NIBRS data collection format.

Table 1: UCR Participation via the NIBRS, by Year					
	Year of Incident				
	2000	2001	2002	2003	2004
United States Population	281,421,906	285,317,559	287,973,924	290,788,976	293,655,404
Percent of US Population Covered by Agencies Reporting via the NIBRS	16%	17%	17%	20%	22%
Number of Agencies Participating in the UCR Program via the NIBRS[1]	3,801	4,259	4,302	5,271	5,735
Percent of Agencies Reporting via the NIBRS	22%	25%	25%	31%	33%
Percent of Crime Reported to the UCR Program via the NIBRS	13%	15%	18%	17%	20%

[1] Based on law enforcement agencies that submitted their UCR data to the FBI in accordance with NIBRS reporting requirements for inclusion in the annual NIBRS database.

Note: See the study text for specific data definitions, uses, and limitations.

Using a combination of six possible data segments (*administrative, offense, victim, property, offender,* and *arrestee*), the NIBRS captures information on criminal incidents involving any of 22 offense categories made up of 46 specific crimes. To date, the NIBRS offers 56 data elements, i.e., data fields, that law enforcement may use to capture descriptive data about the victims, offenders, and circumstances of criminal incidents and arrests.

Examples of NIBRS data elements include *UCR Offense Code, Type of Victim,* and *Age of Offender* (see Appendix E for a complete list of data elements).[9] Furthermore, each of the 56 data elements is translated into a series of codes that specify the information being collected.

Of particular importance to the present study is the NIBRS data element *Location Type,* specifically *Code 22,*[10] which identifies offenses occurring at schools and colleges. All the crime data used in the tables and discussions throughout this study were reported by law enforcement as occurring at NIBRS Location Type, Code 22, which hereafter is referred to as *school(s),* unless otherwise noted.

As illustrated in Figure 1, an incident report contains various types of data collection segments in addition to the administrative segment. The report may also include multiple segment records within one or more segments if the incident should warrant them. For example, an incident occurred during which three victims were held up on school property by two offenders using guns. The offenders shot and killed the victims and were subsequently arrested. This incident will have one administrative record, two offense records, various property records for the stolen or recovered property, three victim records, two offender records, and two arrestee records separated into the appropriate segments in the NIBRS database structure.

This study focuses primarily on the offender and arrestee data records; it looks at other records only as they pertain to offenders. Using the narrowly-defined set of data records, the study specifically addresses incident characteristics (Tables 2 and 7), offender characteristics (Tables 3-5), victim-to-offender relationships (Table 6), offense characteristics (Tables 8 and 9), and arrestee characteristics (Tables 10-15). Expanding Tables 2 and 8, Appendices A and B show the number of offenses by offense type by year and the weapon type by offense type, respectively.

Throughout this study, age groups are aggregated and cross tabulated to help readers view the traits of offenders and arrestees. These age groups are formulated based upon the following age divisions: Birth to 4 years old, 5 to 9 years old, 10 to 12 years old, 13 to 15 years old, 16 to 18 years old, and 19 years or older.

Additional considerations for this study follow:

- The term *gun* refers collectively to all firearm codes found in the NIBRS format, including: firearm, handgun, rifle, shotgun, and other firearm types.[11] Furthermore, information for type weapon/force involved is only collected for *Murder and Nonnegligent Manslaughter, Negligent Manslaughter, Justifiable Homicide, Kidnapping/Abduction, Forcible Rape, Forcible Sodomy, Sexual Assault with an Object, Forcible Fondling, Robbery, Aggravated Assault, Simple Assault, Extortion/Blackmail,* and *Weapon Law Violations.*

- Victim-to-offender relationships are only collected for *Murder and Nonnegligent Manslaughter, Negligent Manslaughter, Justifiable Homicide, Kidnapping/Abduction, Forcible Rape, Forcible Sodomy, Sexual Assault with an Object, Forcible Fondling, Robbery, Aggravated Assault, Simple Assault, Intimidation, Incest,* and *Statutory Rape.*

---

[9] NIBRS Volume 1: *Data Collection Guidelines*, Federal Bureau of Investigation, August 2000.

[10] Technical note for those who wish to replicate the study: NIBRS Data Element #9–Location Type, Code 22–School/College (includes university).

[11] Technical note for those who wish to replicate the study: NIBRS Data Element #13–Weapon/Force Involved, Weapon Type Codes 11, 12, 13, 14, and 15, respectively.

FIGURE 1—Incident Reports to Segments

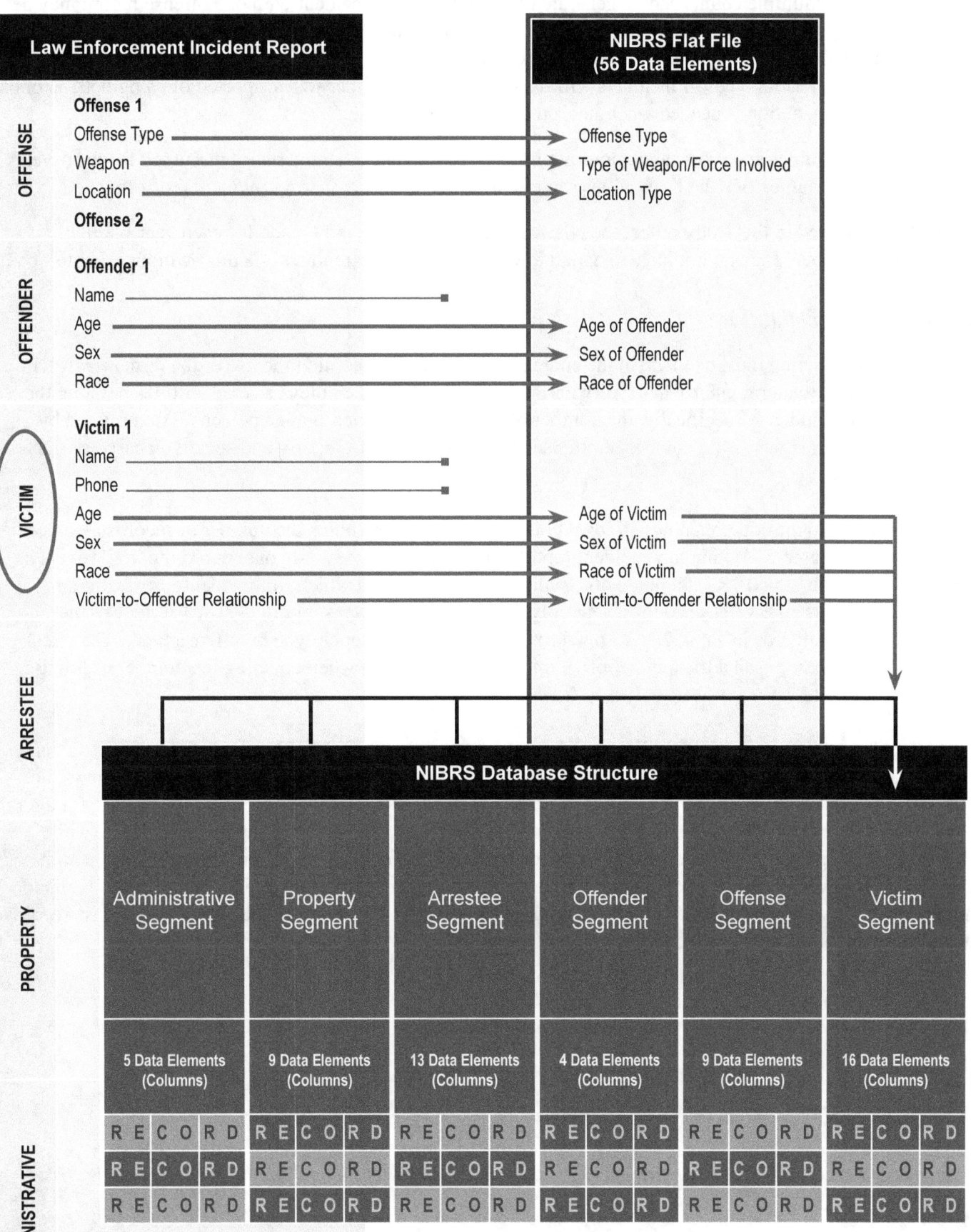

This graphic sample illustrates the extraction of the Victim data elements from the Incident Report to the NIBRS Flat File and how they are segmented into the NIBRS Database Structure.

- Offenders may be suspected of using alcohol, computers, and/or drugs in an offense. Because more than one of these codes can be collected on any given offense record, there may be multiple counts of use in incidents. Multiple counts can be generated in two ways. An incident with one offense record may be associated with the use of alcohol and drugs. Another incident may contain two offense records, one offense indicating the suspected use of alcohol and a second offense where the offender is suspected of using drugs. Both types of incidents will indicate that the offender was suspected of using both alcohol and drugs. Caution is needed when interpreting this information.

- Frequency tables and cross tabulations are used to examine the characteristics discussed for the 5-year study time frame. See the Limitations section on cautions for comparing frequencies from year to year.

- The data used in this study reflect the NIBRS submissions originally made for each year within the 5-year period. They do not include data that were subsequently reported via time-window submissions.[12]

Special Offense Definitions

An important distinction must be made in the context of this study concerning the use of the term *offense*. In the UCR Program, the term *offense* has a very particular definition that employs a series of rules defining the way offenses are counted. Specifically, the number of offenses for crimes against persons is determined by the number of victims, while the number of offenses for crimes against property and society is based on each distinct operation.

This study also introduces a nontraditional counting method that counts the number of records associated with the offense segment. Within any incident reported in NIBRS, there is only one record reported for each unique offense code. In NIBRS, there are 46 Group A offense codes in which full incident information is collected and 11 Group B offense codes where only arrestee information is reported. This study uses the number of offense records in Table 2 and Appendix B which shows weapon type by offense type. The effect of this counting method is that the number of victims is not considered when counting the number of offense records. (See Figure 2.)

Figure 2, on the following page, illustrates how offenses and offense records are counted in NIBRS for a hypothetical incident with three victims of homicide who were also robbed. The left of the figure shows the counts of offenses which include three counts of homicide, *Code 09A,* and one of robbery, *Code 120*, for a total of four offenses. Because homicide is a crime against persons, one offense is tallied for each victim, while robbery, a crime against property, only counts one offense for each distinct operation, regardless of the number of victims. However, on the right of the figure where offense records are counted, only one count of homicide and one of robbery are used to determine the sum of offense records. Therefore, the number of offense records equals two, one for each unique offense type in this example.

---

[12] Please refer to NIBRS Volume 2: *Data Submission Specifications*, Federal Bureau of Investigation, May 1992, for more details on time-window submissions.

FIGURE 2—Segment Records to Counts

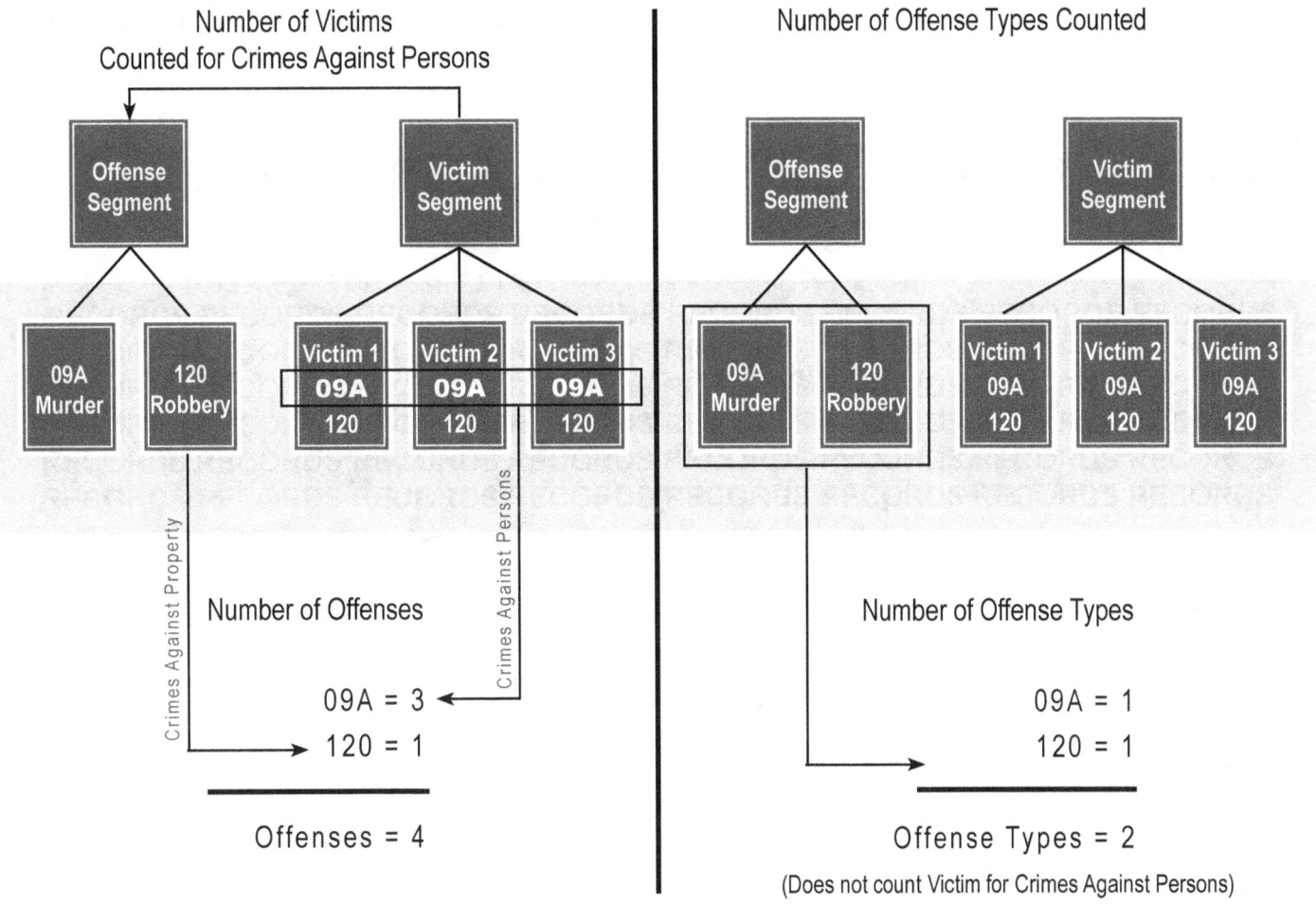

Because this study focuses on offenders and arrestees, this approach is beneficial, particularly when examining weapon type by offense type (see Appendix B), since it eliminates the natural weighting that occurs when using traditional UCR offense counting rules based on the number of victims. For example, because the weapon type is associated with the offense segment in NIBRS, an incident involving three murder victims has three offenses connected to the weapon type, overestimating the presence of that weapon type. However, if the offense type is maintained as the unit of analysis for weapon type, the weighting of weapon types by the number of victims is avoided. Of greater relevance to the objective of this study are the types of offenses that offenders commit in schools. Certainly, studies involving NIBRS data that focus on the victim or offense segments require the examination of offenses based on the traditional UCR offense counting practices.

Analyses and Results

Incident Characteristics

Of the 17,065,074 incidents reported through the NIBRS by law enforcement from 2000 to 2004, 558,219 (3.3 percent) occurred at schools. There were 589,534 offense records, 619,453 offenses, and 688,612 offender records reported in those incidents. The statistics discussed in this report are based on the

476,803 offenders for whom at least one attribute (age, gender, race, and/or number of offenders) was known.[13] However, none of the characteristics for offenders (age, gender, race, or number of offenders) were known in 211,809 of the 688,612 offender records. During these 5 years, there were 181,468 arrestees associated with crime in schools. (See Table 2.) According to UCR guidelines, the arrestee may be different than the person who was reported as the offender.

	Table 2: Overview of Crime in Schools, by Year					
	Year of Incident					
	2000	**2001**	**2002**	**2003**	**2004**	**5-Year Total**
Number of Incidents:						
In all locations	2,616,448	3,269,022	3,458,569	3,684,154	4,036,881	17,065,074
In schools	84,627	109,239	110,467	121,765	132,121	558,219
Percent of Incidents in Schools	3.2	3.3	3.2	3.3	3.3	3.3
Characteristics of Incidents in Schools						
Number of Offenses	92,242	120,938	123,200	135,489	147,584	619,453
Offense Records	88,687	115,642	117,341	128,542	139,322	589,534
Offender Records[1]	102,655	134,088	136,358	150,913	164,598	688,612
Unknown Offender Records[2]	33,239	42,784	41,761	46,106	47,919	211,809
Persons Arrested	24,662	33,280	34,360	41,057	48,109	181,468

[1] Includes the number of *unknown offender* records.
[2] *Unknown offender* records are reported when nothing is known about the offenders in the incident, including age, gender, race, and number of offender(s). See p. 99 of NIBRS Volume 1: *Data Collection Guidelines*, August 2000, for more details.

Note: See the study text for specific data definitions, uses, and limitations.

Offender Characteristics

Age was known for 393,938 offenders.[14] Of those, most (38.0 percent) were 13-15 year olds. The second largest group was 16-18 year olds (30.7 percent), followed by those offenders aged 19 or older (18.2 percent) and 10-12 year olds (11.0 percent). Offenders 9 years old or under accounted for 2.1 percent of the offenders where the age was known. By looking at only those offenders for whom the age was known, offenders 18 years of age or younger were 4.5 times more likely to be involved in crime at schools than older offenders. There were 82,865 offenders for whom the age was unknown (but other characteristics, such as gender and/or race, were known to the police). (Based on Table 3.)

---

[13] The term *known offender* does not imply that the identity of the suspect is known, but only that a characteristic of the suspect has been identified, which distinguishes him/her from an unknown offender.

[14] Law enforcement may report a range of ages. NIBRS reports the midpoint of the age range (e.g., offender age 25-35 is reported as 30).

Table 3: Offenders[1] of Crime in Schools, by Age[2], by Year

Age (Years)	Year of Incident					5-Year Total
	2000	2001	2002	2003	2004	
0–4	35	49	74	53	76	287
5–9	1,246	1,807	1,521	1,563	1,775	7,912
10–12	5,845	8,541	8,859	9,557	10,640	43,442
13–15	20,244	28,171	29,697	33,163	38,347	149,622
16–18	16,732	22,506	23,564	27,533	30,624	120,959
19 or Older	10,748	13,608	14,295	15,637	17,428	71,716
Unknown Age[1]	14,566	16,622	16,587	17,301	17,789	82,865
Total Offenders[3]	69,416	91,304	94,597	104,807	116,679	476,803

[1] At least one other characteristic (gender, race, or number of offenders) was reported.
[2] Law enforcement may report a range of ages. NIBRS reports the midpoint of the age range (e.g., offender age 25-35 is reported as 30).
[3] Over the 5-year study period, there were 211,809 offenders for whom the age, gender, race, and number of offenders were not reported.

Note: See the study text for specific data definitions, uses, and limitations.

For the 5-year study period, the majority (313,556 or 76.7 percent) of the offenders about whom gender was known were males, who were reported as offenders 3.3 times more often than females. Of the offenders for whom age, race, and/or number of offenders was known, the gender was unknown to law enforcement for 67,796 offenders (14.2 percent). (Based on Table 4.)

Table 4: Offenders[1] of Crime in Schools, by Gender, by Year

Gender	Year of Incident					5-Year Total
	2000	2001	2002	2003	2004	
Male	45,011	60,358	61,831	69,288	77,068	313,556
Female	12,560	17,471	18,876	21,248	25,296	95,451
Unknown Gender[1]	11,845	13,475	13,890	14,271	14,315	67,796
Total Offenders[2]	69,416	91,304	94,597	104,807	116,679	476,803

[1] At least one other characteristic (age, race, or number of offenders) was reported.
[2] Over the 5-year study period, there were 211,809 offenders for whom the age, gender, race, and number of offenders were not reported.

Note: See the study text for specific data definitions, uses, and limitations.

Of the 394,173 offenders about whom race was known, white offenders accounted for 71.1 percent (280,178); black offenders, 27.4 percent (107,878); and all other races combined, less than 2 percent (6,117).[15] When race was known, whites were 2.5 times more likely to be reported as an offender at a school than were all other races combined. Of the total offenders about whom age and/or gender were known (476,803), race was unknown for 17.3 percent. (Based on Table 5.)

	Table 5: Offenders[1] of Crime in Schools, by Race, by Year					
	Year of Incident					
Race	2000	2001	2002	2003	2004	5-Year Total
White	41,220	53,862	55,735	61,849	67,512	280,178
Black	13,319	19,876	20,918	24,225	29,540	107,878
Asian/Pacific Islander	584	783	767	936	915	3,985
American Indian/ Alaskan Native	282	359	432	433	626	2,132
Unknown Race[1]	14,011	16,424	16,745	17,364	18,086	82,630
Total Offenders[2]	69,416	91,304	94,597	104,807	116,679	476,803

[1] At least one other characteristic (age, gender, or number of offenders) was reported.
[2] Over the 5-year study period, there were 211,809 offenders for whom the age, gender, race, and number of offenders were not reported.

Note: See the study text for specific data definitions, uses, and limitations.

Victim-to-Offender Relationships

Table 6 provides breakdowns for victim-to-offender relationships, an important aspect to understand when examining crime at schools. It is also important to understand the information in Table 6 reflects a count of relationships and not merely the number of victims and/or offenders. For example, if an incident has four victims and two offenders, there are eight relationship pairings noted in the table (4 victims multiplied by 2 offenders equals 8 relationships).

By far, the relationship type most often reported for crime in schools was *Acquaintance*, with 107,533 instances occurring during the 5-year study period. When *Acquaintance* was combined with the *Otherwise Known* category (50,486 instances), these two categories were 3.3 times more likely to occur as the relationship than were all other victim-to-offender relationships in which the relationship was known. The relationship *Victim was Offender* was reported for 15,539 occurrences, or 7.5 percent of known relationships. This type of relationship is one in which all participants in the incidents were victims and offenders of the same offense, such as assaults being reported as a result of a brawl or fight.[16] *Stranger* was reported for 7.5 percent (15,511 instances) of the relationships. The remaining percentages were widely dispersed among all other relationship categories.

---

[15] UCR race reporting guidelines for NIBRS Data Element #39–*Race (of offender)* follow the minimally accepted standards established by OMB Directive 15. The NIBRS guidelines can be found in NIBRS Volume 1: *Data Collection Guidelines*, Federal Bureau of Investigation, August 2000, p. 100.

[16] *UCR Handbook*, NIBRS Edition, Federal Bureau of Investigation, 1992.

Table 6: Relationship[1] of Victims to Offenders of Crime in Schools, by Year

Relationship (Victim was . . .)	Year of Incident					5-Year Total
	2000	2001	2002	2003	2004	
Acquaintance	14,074	20,429	22,102	23,647	27,281	107,533
Otherwise Known	6,326	8,960	9,845	11,192	14,163	50,486
Victim was Offender[2]	1,429	2,805	3,173	3,543	4,589	15,539
Stranger	2,301	3,060	3,045	3,405	3,700	15,511
Friend	1,300	1,465	1,719	1,501	2,006	7,991
Boyfriend/Girlfriend	452	609	600	741	888	3,290
Child	187	220	266	245	326	1,244
Spouse	117	162	155	170	163	767
Other Family Member	117	111	112	131	159	630
Neighbor	110	91	94	116	130	541
Sibling	84	76	102	124	144	530
Parent	66	96	95	79	141	477
Employee	44	76	69	103	146	438
Ex-Spouse	54	67	84	95	78	378
Employer	28	32	43	33	43	179
Babysittee (the baby)	26	23	25	23	26	123
In-Law	10	26	25	27	32	120
Stepchild	12	28	15	22	23	100
Child of Boyfriend/Girlfriend	14	6	14	14	19	67
Stepparent	12	14	15	11	13	65
Homosexual Relationship	2	7	9	16	30	64
Common-Law Spouse	7	18	11	10	16	62
Grandchild	9	7	5	12	15	48
Stepsibling	6	4	10	15	6	41
Grandparent	0	6	5	6	9	26
Relationship Unknown	4,752	7,089	7,184	7,815	8,721	35,561
Total Relationships[1]	**31,539**	**45,487**	**48,822**	**53,096**	**62,867**	**241,811**

[1] There is not a 1:1 correspondence of relationships to incidents. For example, if an incident has 4 victims and 2 offenders, 8 relationship pairings are noted (4 victims multiplied by 2 offenders equals 8 relationships).

[2] *Victim was Offender* is a relationship in which all participants in the incidents were victims and offenders of the same offense, such as assaults being reported as a result of a brawl or fight.

Note: See the study text for specific data definitions, uses, and limitations.

Offense Characteristics

A rich level of detail about offense characteristics is captured in the NIBRS format. Of particular interest for the present study is the month of occurrence/report, use of weapons/force, and suspected use of alcohol, computers, and/or drugs by offenders.[17]

Table 7 provides the number of incidents as they were reported by month for each year of the study. The month with the most incidents for the 5-year period was October, with a total of 66,726. Among the 5-year totals, the month of March had the second-highest number of reported incidents (58,363), and September followed with 57,417 incidents. It should be noted, however, that on some occasions, the date of the incident is unknown to law enforcement.[18] For example, a school principal notices vandalism at the school on Monday morning and reports the crime. Though the principal knows the vandalism did not occur before Friday afternoon, neither he nor law enforcement can determine whether it happened Friday evening, Saturday, Sunday, or

	Year of Incident					Incident Dates 5-Year Total	Report Dates 5-Year Total
Month	**2000**	**2001**	**2002**	**2003**	**2004**		
January	6,660	9,275	9,717	10,010	10,610	46,272	9,160
February	8,316	9,781	10,394	10,168	12,808	51,467	9,794
March	9,069	12,056	10,362	12,393	14,483	58,363	11,739
April	7,739	10,520	11,058	12,462	13,038	54,817	10,287
May	8,230	10,920	11,050	12,297	12,337	54,834	10,883
June	4,527	5,187	4,901	5,992	6,019	26,626	5,705
July	3,102	3,880	3,894	4,213	4,245	19,334	4,132
August	4,093	5,167	5,267	5,556	6,063	26,146	4,615
September	8,814	10,539	11,490	12,852	13,722	57,417	10,888
October	10,136	12,919	13,183	15,192	15,296	66,726	12,893
November	8,090	10,553	10,829	11,264	13,178	53,914	10,538
December	5,851	8,442	8,322	9,366	10,322	42,303	7,994
Total Incidents	**84,627**	**109,239**	**110,467**	**121,765**	**132,121**	**558,219**	**108,628**

Table 7: Incident and Report Date of Crime in Schools by Month, by Year

Note: Report date counts are included in incident date totals. See the study text for specific data definitions, uses, and limitations.

---

[17] These three items are collected jointly in the NIBRS. Refer to p. 38 of the *UCR Handbook*, NIBRS Edition, Federal Bureau of Investigation, 1992, for a detailed explanation and examples of how these items could be used in the perpetration of a crime.

[18] NIBRS Volume 1: *Data Collection Guidelines*, Federal Bureau of Investigation, August 2000, p. 69.

early Monday morning. Therefore, law enforcement reports the earliest date in which the incident could have occurred (Friday) as the date of the incident. In other instances, a crime occurs during a holiday or summer break and is not discovered and reported until the start of school or after the change of a month. Law enforcement enters the date of the report as the date of the incident, potentially counting the incident in a different month than when it occurred. In this study, incidents in which the dates of reports were used accounted for 19.5 percent of the incidents reported as having occurred in school locations. However, the percentages by month for the dates of reports and the actual dates of incidents are very similar (within 0.5 percent for each month), which indicates that only a small percentage of incidents may have occurred in prior months.

The particular types of weapons/force used are shown in Table 8.[19] The most common weapon type reported was personal weapons (the offender's hands, fists, feet, etc.), which were reported 98,394 times. Personal weapons were 3.4 times more likely to have been reported than any other weapon type (excluding *None* and *Unknown*). The weapon type *None* was reported 16,260 times in the study, which is relatively large compared to the other known weapon types. See the table in Appendix B for a cross-table of weapon type by offense type.

Table 8: Type of Weapon/Force Used in Crime in Schools, by Year

Weapon Type/Force Used	Year of Incident					5-Year Total
	2000	2001	2002	2003	2004	
Personal Weapons	12,945	17,830	20,636	21,933	25,050	98,394
None	2,702	3,114	2,974	3,294	4,176	16,260
Other	1,775	2,311	2,332	2,420	2,842	11,680
Knife/Cutting Instrument	1,511	2,082	2,080	2,445	2,852	10,970
Handgun	307	376	398	430	497	2,008
Blunt Object	283	404	394	455	469	2,005
Firearm (type not stated)	94	131	103	135	146	609
Other Firearm	74	107	92	155	154	582
Explosives	145	139	93	89	95	561
Motor Vehicle	43	52	46	59	71	271
Fire/Incendiary Device	36	34	42	36	88	236
Rifle	23	33	33	24	37	150
Shotgun	15	24	30	19	24	112
Drugs/Narcotics/Sleeping Pills	9	4	8	14	6	41
Poison	1	8	4	11	16	40
Asphyxiation	2	1	3	6	2	14
Unknown	593	1,128	1,163	1,069	1,098	5,051

Note: See the study text for specific data definitions, uses, and limitations.

---

[19] Weapon types are only reported for *murder and nonnegligent manslaughter, negligent homicide, justifiable homicide, kidnapping, forcible rape, forcible sodomy, sexual assault with an object, forcible fondling, robbery, aggravated assault, extortion,* and *weapon law violations. UCR Handbook,* NIBRS Edition, Federal Bureau of Investigation, 1992.

Of the 3,461 times guns were reportedly used, handguns were most often reported (58.0 percent).[20] Knives/cutting instruments were reportedly used 10,970 times, which outweighs the number of times guns were used by 3.2 to 1. Law enforcement reported the weapon type *Other* 11,680 times.[21] This is quite significant when compared to specific weapon types; however, NIBRS data cannot indicate what types of weapons would fit into this category. The *Other* weapon category may contain, for example, acid, pepper spray, belts, deadly diseases, scalding hot water, or other weapon types not covered by the NIBRS weapon type codes.

Table 9 provides the reported instances in each offense record in which the offenders were suspected of using alcohol, computers, and/or drugs.[22] The data show that such use was minimal in situations occurring at schools during the 5-year study period. Of the 589,534 offense records, reports of offenders suspected of using drugs totaled 32,366, while reports of alcohol use totaled 5,844. Suspected computer use by offenders was reported for 1,655 instances. The offender's suspected use of one or more of these items may have occurred during or shortly before the incident, and the use may have occurred in another location.

Table 9: Reports of Offenders Suspected of Using Alcohol, Computers and/or Drugs in Crime in Schools, by Year

Use Category	Year of Incident					5-Year Total
	2000	2001	2002	2003	2004	
Alcohol	998	1,134	1,154	1,212	1,346	5,844
Computer Equipment	376	409	306	256	308	1,655
Drugs/ Narcotics	4,478	6,233	6,146	7,253	8,256	32,366
Not Applicable	83,194	108,315	110,051	120,163	129,745	551,468

Note: See the study text for specific data definitions, uses, and limitations.

Arrestee Characteristics

In addition to the exploration of offenders, it is also important to examine the characteristics of the arrestees associated with crimes in schools. Though 211,809 offender reports for the 5-year study period were such that age, gender, race, and number of offenders were not reported, some or all of these characteristics were available for 181,468 persons arrested for offenses that occurred at schools. (See Table 2.)

Table 10 shows the offense for which the arrestee was apprehended. The most common offense code reported in arrestee records was simple assault–a crime against persons, followed by drug/narcotic violations–a crime against society. These two arrest offense codes were reportedly associated with more than half (52.2 percent) of the total arrestees. Destruction/damage/vandalism of property accounted for a relatively small

---

[20] Summing the *gun* categories will not yield the number of incidents with guns as there may be more than one gun type in an incident. For example, an incident may have involved the use of a rifle and a shotgun.

[21] The *Other* weapon type is an umbrella category that captures weapon types not reflected in the specific weapon type definitions.

[22] One or more of the offenders may have used the type indicated and one or more offenders may have used more than one type in the same offense. It should also be noted that if an offender used a type in an incident with multiple offenses, its use will be counted in the table more than once.

Table 10: Arrestees of Crime in Schools, by Offense, by Year

Offense	Year of Incident					5-Year Total
	2000	2001	2002	2003	2004	
Crimes Against Persons:						
Simple Assault	6,436	9,136	10,120	11,550	14,220	51,462
Intimidation	830	1,631	1,327	1,434	1,776	6,998
Aggravated Assault	1,009	1,228	1,291	1,427	1,531	6,486
Forcible Fondling	231	300	357	341	446	1,675
Kidnapping/Abduction	43	66	78	80	107	374
Forcible Rape	48	55	31	65	60	259
Sexual Assault With An Object	12	10	34	26	36	118
Forcible Sodomy	19	20	23	20	22	104
Statutory Rape	9	13	11	16	30	79
Murder and Nonnegligent Manslaughter	1	7	7	7	5	27
Incest	0	0	5	2	5	12
Negligent Manslaughter	0	0	0	3	0	3
Crimes Against Property:						
Destruction/Damage/Vandalism of Property	1,755	2,141	2,210	2,665	3,138	11,909
All Other Larceny	1,579	2,004	2,004	2,336	2,689	10,612
Burglary/Breaking and Entering	1,430	1,679	1,698	2,130	2,066	9,003
Theft From Building	1,188	1,387	1,440	1,845	1,973	7,833
Stolen Property Offenses	213	256	313	434	476	1,692
Arson	217	234	253	298	356	1,358
Theft From Motor Vehicle	183	205	208	288	274	1,158
Counterfeiting/Forgery	144	210	209	204	207	974
Shoplifting	124	176	165	165	217	847
Motor Vehicle Theft	144	136	182	195	166	823
Robbery	104	144	163	200	191	802
False Pretenses/Swindle/Confidence Game	59	90	155	85	116	505
Impersonation	52	71	120	67	124	434
Theft From Coin-Operated Machine or Device	71	101	80	54	87	393
Theft of Motor Vehicle Parts or Accessories	58	79	56	73	65	331
Credit Card/Automatic Teller Machine Fraud	38	47	42	51	43	221
Embezzlement	29	41	37	62	45	214
Pocket-Picking	33	30	36	33	38	170

Table 10: Arrestees of Crime in Schools, by Offense (continued)

Offense	Year of Incident					5-Year Total
	2000	2001	2002	2003	2004	
Purse-Snatching	18	25	22	38	41	144
Extortion/Blackmail	15	32	22	12	29	110
Wire Fraud	2	2	3	4	8	19
Bad Checks	0	2	4	2	2	10
Bribery	1	1	0	3	3	8
Crimes Against Society:						
Drug/Narcotic Violations	5,819	7,860	7,850	9,949	11,816	43,294
Weapon Law Violations	1,219	1,625	1,510	1,872	2,297	8,523
Drug Equipment Violations	717	1,030	967	1,123	1,271	5,108
Disorderly Conduct	194	496	557	751	947	2,945
Trespass of Real Property	79	121	118	192	186	696
Liquor Law Violations	82	123	74	158	157	594
Drunkenness	24	28	50	46	54	202
Pornography/Obscene Material	20	34	49	16	36	155
Driving Under the Influence	9	16	18	27	25	95
Curfew/Loitering/Vagrancy Violations	15	10	25	30	14	94
Betting/Wagering	2	2	13	19	19	55
Prostitution	2	5	4	5	6	22
Operating/Promoting/Assisting Gambling	0	12	0	7	0	19
Gambling Equipment Violations	0	10	2	7	0	19
Family Offenses, Nonviolent	0	0	2	7	9	18
Assisting or Promoting Prostitution	0	0	0	5	1	6
Crimes Against Persons, Property, and Society:						
All Other Offenses	358	330	410	621	674	2,393
Non-Crime:						
Runaway	27	19	5	7	5	63
Total Persons Arrested	**24,662**	**33,280**	**34,360**	**41,057**	**48,109**	**181,468**

Note: See the study text for specific data definitions, uses, and limitations.

portion of arrestees (6.6 percent). All other larceny and burglary, both crimes against property, involved 5.8 and 5.0 percent of the arrestees, respectively. Each of the remaining arrest offense codes accounted for less than 5.0 percent of the arrestees. Note that the arrest code does not necessarily match any of the offense codes in an offense segment in the same incident.

The largest group of arrestees about whom the age[23] was known (41.8 percent) was 13 to 15 year olds. Arrestees who were 16 to 18 years old accounted for 32.7 percent; 19 or older, 14.2 percent; 10 to 12 years old, 10.2 percent; and 5 to 9 years old, 1.1 percent. Twelve arrestees who committed crimes at schools were reportedly age 4 or under.[24] For those arrestees about whom the age was known, arrestees were 6.0 times more likely to be 18 years of age or younger than to be 19 years of age or older. The age was unknown for 171 of the arrestees. (Based on Table 11.)

Table 11: Arrestees of Crime in Schools, by Age[1], by Year

Age (Years)	Year of Incident					5-Year Total
	2000	2001	2002	2003	2004	
0–4	2	3	0	3	4	12
5–9	358	472	410	376	412	2,028
10–12	2,494	3,539	3,607	4,093	4,672	18,405
13–15	10,138	13,960	14,351	17,107	20,266	75,822
16–18	7,863	10,609	10,987	13,726	16,052	59,237
19 or Older	3,770	4,644	4,980	5,726	6,673	25,793
Unknown Age	37	53	25	26	30	171
Total Arrestees	24,662	33,280	34,360	41,057	48,109	181,468

[1] Law enforcement may report a range of ages. NIBRS reports the midpoint of the age range (e.g., offender age 25-35 is reported as 30).

Note: See the study text for specific data definitions, uses, and limitations.

During the 5-year period, 78.2 percent of the 181,468 arrestees were males, who were 3.6 times more likely to be arrested than females. (Based on Table 12.)

Table 12: Arrestees of Crime in Schools, by Gender, by Year

Gender	Year of Incident					5-Year Total
	2000	2001	2002	2003	2004	
Male	19,717	26,343	26,812	32,146	36,868	141,886
Female	4,945	6,937	7,548	8,911	11,241	39,582
Total Arrestees	24,662	33,280	34,360	41,057	48,109	181,468

Note: See the study text for specific data definitions, uses, and limitations.

---

[23] Law enforcement may report a range of ages. NIBRS reports the midpoint of the age range (e.g., offender age 25-35 is reported as 30).

[24] These data were not tested for validity and are presented as they are found in the NIBRS database. Please see the Limitations section for more details.

Of the 179,109 arrestees about whom the race was known, 72.8 percent were white; 25.3 percent were black; and 1.9 percent were all other race categories combined. White was 2.7 times more likely to be reported as the arrestee race than were any of the other race categories. A total of 2,359 arrestees were reported with an unknown race. (Based on Table 13.)

Table 13: Arrestees of Crime in Schools, by Race, by Year

Race	Year of Incident					5-Year Total
	2000	2001	2002	2003	2004	
White	18,589	24,194	24,943	29,084	33,518	130,328
Black	5,308	8,032	8,274	10,663	13,077	45,354
Asian/Pacific Islander	277	410	383	523	521	2,114
American Indian/Alaskan Native	171	232	289	268	353	1,313
Unknown Race	317	412	471	519	640	2,359
Total Arrestees	24,662	33,280	34,360	41,057	48,109	181,468

Note: See the study text for specific data definitions, uses, and limitations.

Law enforcement agencies submitting NIBRS data are not required to report the ethnicity of the arrestee to the FBI. Of the 136,957 arrestees about whom ethnicity was known and reported, 89.4 percent were non-Hispanic. Excluding unknown ethnicity, arrestees were 8.4 times more likely to be non-Hispanic. (Based on Table 14.) There were 18,208 arrestees about whom the ethnicity status was not reported during the 5-year study period.

Table 14: Arrestees[1] of Crime in Schools, by Ethnicity, by Year

Ethnicity	Year of Incident					5-Year Total
	2000	2001	2002	2003	2004	
Hispanic	1,729	2,439	2,862	3,439	4,103	14,572
Non-Hispanic	16,791	22,783	23,631	27,638	31,542	122,385
Unknown Ethnicity	3,793	4,440	4,631	5,820	7,619	26,303
Total Arrestees[1]	22,313	29,662	31,124	36,897	43,264	163,260

[1] Over the 5-year study period, there were 18,208 arrestees for whom the ethnicity was not reported.

Note: See the study text for specific data definitions, uses, and limitations.

As with supplying the ethnicity of an arrestee, providing resident status for an arrestee is an optional reporting field in the NIBRS. For the purpose of this study, a resident is a person who maintains his/her permanent home for legal purposes in the locality (that is, town, city, or community) where the school is located and in which the crime occurred.[25] Of the 145,339 arrestees about whom resident status was known and reported, 79.2 percent were residents. When the resident status was known, arrestees were nearly 3.8 times more likely to be residents of the community in which the crime took place. (Based on Table 15.) During the 5 years of data submissions from 2000 to 2004, there were 17,767 arrestees about whom resident status was not reported to the UCR Program.

Table 15: Arrestees[1] of Crime in Schools, by Resident Status, by Year

Resident Status	Year of Incident					5-Year Total
	2000	2001	2002	2003	2004	
Resident[2]	15,367	20,661	21,609	26,294	31,112	115,043
Nonresident	4,278	5,686	5,768	6,811	7,753	30,296
Unknown Residence	2,263	3,155	3,193	4,294	5,457	18,362
Total Arrestees[1]	21,908	29,502	30,570	37,399	44,322	163,701

[1] Over the 5-year study period, there were 17,767 arrestees for whom the resident status was not reported.

[2] A *resident* is a person who maintains his/her permanent home for legal purposes in the locality (i.e., town, city, or community) where the crime took place.

Note: See the study text for specific data definitions, uses, and limitations.

Limitations

Studies that use NIBRS data have inherent limitations. First, when the NIBRS data show increases in crime over a period of years, it should not be assumed that the volume of criminal incidents in the Nation actually increased. As seen in Table 1, such apparent increases from year to year may well be the result of increases in the number of law enforcement agencies (1,934 more agencies over the 5-year period) reporting their UCR data via the NIBRS format. As the percentage of agencies participating in the UCR Program via the NIBRS increases and the NIBRS data become more representative of crime nationwide, data analysts will be better equipped to identify increases and decreases in crime that are due to actual changes in crime volume rather than to reporting. Furthermore, changes in proportions between groups should not be interpreted as an actual change in the Nation's crime characteristics. It is possible that demographics of the new reporting agencies are influencing the proportion (e.g., should the data show a sharp increase in the percentage of one particular race of offender between two years). As more law enforcement agencies report via the NIBRS, analysts will be more confident that the demographic characteristics of the data can be considered nationally representative. It is expected that, eventually, the NIBRS data, combined with other exogenous datasets, will allow researchers to evaluate the effect of crime reduction policies in reducing crime. Another potential limitation is that the agencies that submit their UCR data via the NIBRS format are not, for the most part, in large metropolitan areas. In spite of these limitations, there have been studies that suggest that the NIBRS data may be representative of the Nation's crime (see, for example, Section V of *Crime in the United States, 2002*, "Bank Robbery in the United States").

Another limitation of studies that use NIBRS data stems from the restricting level of disaggregation possible when using NIBRS location codes. For example, crimes committed at school, college, and university locations are all combined into a single NIBRS location code. Separating elementary and secondary schools

---

[25] NIBRS Volume 1: *Data Collection Guidelines*, Federal Bureau of Investigation, August 2000, p. 104.

from colleges is difficult, if not impossible, in the NIBRS format. The parameters available in NIBRS that might help distinguish whether an incident took place at an elementary school, secondary school, or college are not mutually exclusive to any group. For example, there are many 17 year olds in college and, conversely, many 18 year olds in high school during the same period of time; therefore, age of victim, offender, or arrestee are not variables that can identify whether the incident occurred in an elementary school, secondary school, or college. In addition, neither the victim nor the offender necessarily attends the institution where the offense occurred.

Lastly, the validity of NIBRS data has not been tested; therefore, one should be cautious in the interpretation of surprising findings, e.g., twelve 0-4 year old arrestees. (See Table 11.) However, since one purpose of this study is to show the arrestee and offender information that can be gleaned from incidents involving crime in school locations reported via the NIBRS, data such as these are included in the study.

Because of these limitations, the findings discussed in the present study cannot be generalized to the Nation as a whole. Readers are advised to be cautious in applying the results of this study to other research.

Summary and Conclusions

In summary, this study, over the 5-year period, found that 3.3 percent of all incidents reported via NIBRS involved school locations. The number of crime in school-related incidents was highest in October. Offense records were also most likely to include the use of personal weapons (hands, fists, feet, etc.), while reports of the offender's use of alcohol, computers, and/or drugs were minimal. Reported offenders of crime in schools were most likely 13-15 year old white males who the victims reportedly knew; however, there was nearly an equally large number of 16-18 year old reported offenders. More than half of the arrestees associated with crime at school locations were arrested for simple assault or drug/narcotic violations. Arrestees had similar characteristics to the reported offenders, most likely being reported as 13-15 year old white non-Hispanic males who were residents of the community of the school location where the incident was reported.

As a society, we are concerned by crime in schools and driven by the need for better data and analyses that can be used to develop protections for these institutions and the people who use their services. When more agencies use the NIBRS format to report UCR data, the data will allow for statistical estimations and tests.

Future studies using the rich NIBRS dataset may look at incident, offense, victim, and property characteristics; regional and rural/urban differences; as well as other socioeconomic and demographic considerations, such as:

- Comparisons to other crime in school databases such as the Department of Education or other agencies.
- NIBRS data validity (e.g., explaining the twelve 0-4 year old arrestees).
- Various victim, offender, or offense rates based on population.

Incident Characteristics
- Exceptional Clearances of crimes in schools.
- Crime in schools by region.
- Differences in crime in schools between urban vs. rural settings.
- Association of time of day to incidents.
- Month of incident (April as compared to others for "rampage" homicides like Columbine and Virginia Tech).

Offense Characteristics

- Hate crime in schools.
- Attempted versus completed crimes.
- Type of criminal activity or gang information.

Victim Characteristics

- Victims by age, gender, and race.
- Types of victim injury in violence in schools.
- Age differences between victims and offenders.
- Incidents involving single victims and offenders.

Property Characteristics

- Type of property loss associated with incidents at schools.
- Description of property type involved.
- Value of property in crime in schools.
- Type and quantity of drugs.

By extracting relevant data elements from the NIBRS portion of the UCR databases, and by presenting percentages and odds ratios for characteristic differences among offenders and arrestees, this study sheds light on identifying the characteristics of offenders and arrestees of crimes at schools. Statistics presented here do not identify the factors of crime in schools. However, the study is an example of the way in which the NIBRS data can be used to explore facets of seemingly difficult problems and to generate questions and further research. This study adds to the body of research concerning crime in schools and particularly the often overlooked categories of school-related property and society crimes. One aim of school officials and law enforcement is to reduce crime in schools in general. As such, the findings presented here may be useful for those officials and policy makers at educational institutions who are seeking to develop proactive policies, an important need to effectively protect these vital societal foundations.

Appendix A: Number of Offenses of Crime in Schools, by Offense Type, by Year

Offense	Year of Incident					5-Year Total
	2000	2001	2002	2003	2004	
Crimes Against Persons:						
Simple Assault	16,898	23,614	26,587	29,015	33,561	129,675
Intimidation	5,154	8,340	6,792	7,164	8,265	35,715
Aggravated Assault	2,417	2,920	3,092	3,235	3,634	15,298
Forcible Fondling	1,148	1,479	1,745	1,736	2,085	8,193
Forcible Rape	241	301	320	359	441	1,662
Kidnapping/Abduction	153	200	230	278	307	1,168
Forcible Sodomy	74	107	108	123	130	542
Sexual Assault With An Object	75	74	101	111	128	489
Statutory Rape	28	32	45	74	101	280
Murder and Nonnegligent Manslaughter	2	8	14	5	8	37
Incest	0	5	9	5	0	19
Negligent Manslaughter	1	0	0	1	0	2
Crimes Against Property:						
Destruction/Damage/Vandalism of Property	17,593	21,210	20,814	23,017	23,647	106,281
Theft From Building	14,761	18,610	18,983	20,928	20,830	94,112
All Other Larceny	11,478	14,195	14,550	15,945	17,999	74,167
Burglary/Breaking and Entering	4,106	5,482	5,712	6,295	6,733	28,328
Theft From Motor Vehicle	3,281	4,080	3,693	3,727	3,543	18,324
Theft of Motor Vehicle Parts or Accessories	824	1,279	1,250	1,346	1,164	5,863
Motor Vehicle Theft	755	933	954	912	846	4,400
Arson	658	766	760	850	980	4,014
Counterfeiting/Forgery	401	440	523	620	693	2,677
False Pretenses/Swindle/Confidence Game	272	389	470	595	599	2,325
Theft From Coin-Operated Machine or Device	355	442	406	440	469	2,112
Stolen Property Offenses	309	385	395	466	478	2,033
Robbery	241	329	340	371	411	1,692
Credit Card/Automatic Teller Machine Fraud	188	267	276	307	307	1,345
Shoplifting	176	235	232	240	318	1,201

Offense	Year of Incident					5-Year Total
	2000	2001	2002	2003	2004	
Pocket-Picking	152	171	181	245	281	1,030
Embezzlement	175	259	229	194	172	1,029
Purse-Snatching	104	153	201	209	238	905
Impersonation	85	131	165	157	201	739
Extortion/Blackmail	30	40	34	27	50	181
Wire Fraud	17	14	27	17	32	107
Bribery	3	2	1	2	1	9
Welfare Fraud	0	0	0	1	2	3
Crimes Against Society:						
Drug/Narcotic Violations	6,477	8,879	8,845	10,685	12,222	47,108
Weapon Law Violations	2,104	2,806	2,667	3,079	3,715	14,371
Drug Equipment Violations	1,431	2,237	2,310	2,575	2,859	11,412
Pornography/Obscene Material	64	102	102	92	107	467
Betting/Wagering	4	6	13	14	9	46
Gambling Equipment Violations	0	3	9	11	8	31
Prostitution	5	6	5	7	5	28
Operating/Promoting/Assisting Gambling	1	5	7	5	2	20
Assisting or Promoting Prostitution	1	2	3	4	3	13
Sports Tampering	0	0	0	0	0	0
Total Offenses	**92,242**	**120,938**	**123,200**	**135,489**	**147,584**	**619,453**

Appendix B: Weapon Type by Offense Type for Crime in Schools, 2000-2004

Offense	Firearm	Handgun	Rifle	Shotgun	Other Firearm	Knife/Cutting Instrument	Blunt Object	Motor Vehicle	Personal Weapons
Simple Assault	0	0	0	0	0	0	0	0	86,312
Aggravated Assault	130	331	17	11	91	2,185	1,560	261	4,824
Forcible Fondling	1	2	0	1	0	12	5	1	4,454
Forcible Rape	2	15	0	1	0	14	2	1	892
Robbery	53	259	1	11	5	122	28	0	857
Kidnapping/Abduction	9	19	1	2	0	19	1	6	361
Sexual Assault With An Object	0	1	0	1	0	2	4	0	282
Forcible Sodomy	1	1	0	0	1	2	2	0	258
Weapon Law Violations	405	1,371	131	85	485	8,606	401	1	94
Extortion/Blackmail	2	1	0	0	0	4	1	0	58
Murder and Nonnegligent Manslaughter	6	7	0	0	0	4	1	1	2
Negligent Manslaughter	0	0	0	0	0	0	0	0	0
Justifiable Homicide	0	1	0	0	0	0	0	0	0
Total	**609**	**2,008**	**150**	**112**	**582**	**10,970**	**2,005**	**271**	**98,394**

Appendix B: Weapon Type *(continued)*

Offense	Poison	Explosives	Fire/Incendiary Device	Drugs/Narcotics	Asphyxiation	Other	Unknown	None
Simple Assault	0	0	0	0	0	7,899	4,039	11,661
Aggravated Assault	34	20	151	20	11	2,074	249	457
Forcible Fondling	0	0	0	1	0	273	267	1,786
Forcible Rape	0	0	0	9	0	50	93	511
Robbery	0	0	0	0	0	61	72	255
Kidnapping/Abduction	0	1	0	0	0	51	59	320
Sexual Assault With An Object	0	0	0	1	0	32	23	76
Forcible Sodomy	0	0	0	0	1	23	31	155
Weapon Law Violations	6	537	85	9	1	1,199	208	952
Extortion/Blackmail	0	3	0	1	0	18	6	87
Murder and Nonnegligent Manslaughter	0	0	0	0	1	2	3	0
Negligent Manslaughter	0	0	0	0	0	1	1	0
Justifiable Homicide	0	0	0	0	0	0	0	0
Total	**40**	**561**	**236**	**41**	**14**	**11,683**	**5,051**	**16,260**

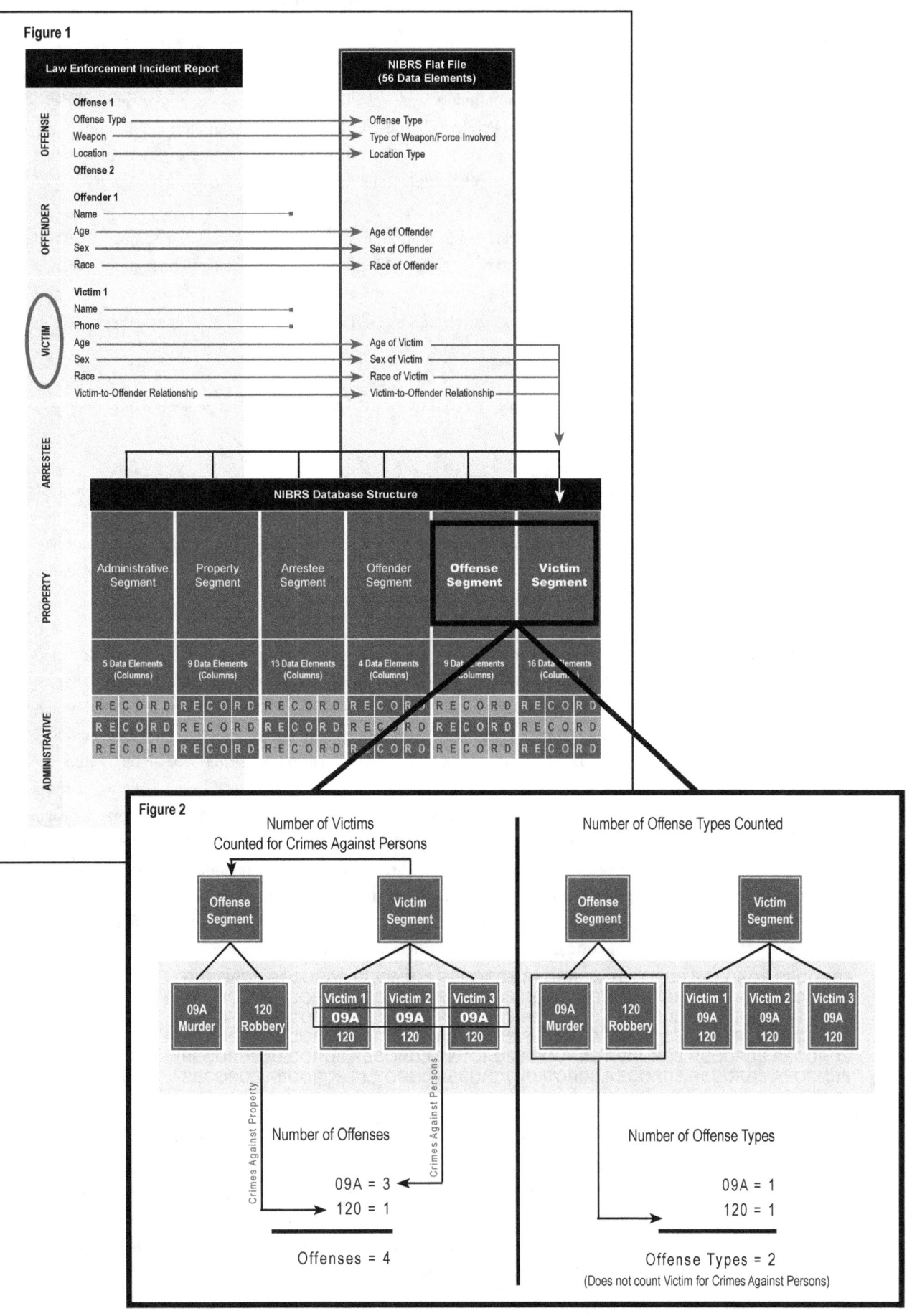

Figure 1

Law Enforcement Incident Report

NIBRS Flat File (56 Data Elements)

OFFENSE

Offense 1
Offense Type → Offense Type
Weapon → Type of Weapon/Force Involved
Location → Location Type
Offense 2

OFFENDER

Offender 1
Name
Age → Age of Offender
Sex → Sex of Offender
Race → Race of Offender

VICTIM

Victim 1
Name
Phone
Age → Age of Victim
Sex → Sex of Victim
Race → Race of Victim
Victim-to-Offender Relationship → Victim-to-Offender Relationship

ARRESTEE

PROPERTY

ADMINISTRATIVE

NIBRS Database Structure

Administrative Segment	Property Segment	Arrestee Segment	Offender Segment	**Offense Segment**	**Victim Segment**
5 Data Elements (Columns)	9 Data Elements (Columns)	13 Data Elements (Columns)	4 Data Elements (Columns)	9 Data Elements (Columns)	16 Data Elements (Columns)
RECORD	RECORD	RECORD	RECORD	RECORD	RECORD
RECORD	RECORD	RECORD	RECORD	RECORD	RECORD
RECORD	RECORD	RECORD	RECORD	RECORD	RECORD

Figure 2

Number of Victims Counted for Crimes Against Persons

Number of Offense Types Counted

Offense Segment
 — 09A Murder
 — 120 Robbery

Victim Segment
 — Victim 1: **09A** / 120
 — Victim 2: **09A** / 120
 — Victim 3: **09A** / 120

Crimes Against Property

Crimes Against Persons

Number of Offenses

09A = 3
120 = 1
———
Offenses = 4

Offense Segment
 — 09A Murder / 120 Robbery

Victim Segment
 — Victim 1: 09A / 120
 — Victim 2: 09A / 120
 — Victim 3: 09A / 120

Number of Offense Types

09A = 1
120 = 1
———
Offense Types = 2
(Does not count Victim for Crimes Against Persons)

25

Appendix D: Table Methodology

Table	Data Used	Construction
1	US Census and UCR	-
2	NIBRS Administrative, Offense, Offender, and Arrestee Segments	ORI and incident numbers were selected in the offense segment where offense location = "school/college." These ORI and incident numbers act as unique identifiers and were matched to the other segments in order to count the selected table fields. The numbers reflect the number of records for each category.
3	NIBRS Offender Segment	Offender ages were collapsed into the given age groups. Each number reflects the number of offenders reported. Offenders were only counted once in the table.
4	NIBRS Offender Segment	Offender genders are selected by NIBRS gender code. Offenders were only counted once in the table.
5	NIBRS Offender Segment	Offender races are selected by NIBRS race code. Offenders were only counted once in the table.
6	NIBRS Victim Segment	Victim-to-offender relationships are determined by victim segment data elements. NIBRS collects relationship information for up to 10 offenders for each victim. The numbers reflected indicate the number of relationships (not just the number of victims or offenders). For example, an incident with 3 victims and 3 offenders involves 6 people but 9 relationships.
7	NIBRS Administrative Segment	The numbers in the table are the number of incidents and report dates associated with school locations by month and year. On some occasions, the date of the incident is unknown to law enforcement. For example, a school principal notices vandalism at the school on Monday morning and reports the crime. Though the principal knows the vandalism did not occur before Friday afternoon, neither he nor law enforcement can determine whether it happened Friday evening, Saturday, Sunday, or early Monday morning. Therefore, law enforcement reports the earliest date in which the incident could have occurred (Friday) as the date of the incident. In other instances, a crime occurs during a holiday or summer break and is not discovered and reported until the start of school or after the change of a month. Law enforcement enters the date of the report as the date of the incident, potentially counting the incident in a different month than when it occurred. In this study, incidents in which the dates of reports were used accounted for 19.5 percent of the incidents reported as having occurred in school locations. However, the percentages by month for the dates of reports and the actual dates of incidents are very similar (within 0.5 percent for each month), which indicates that only a small percentage of incidents may have occurred in prior months.
8	NIBRS Offense Segment	The numbers in the table count the various entries reported for type weapon/force involved within an incident. Though each offense may have up to three types, the table does not count the number of weapons. For example, if three shotguns were used in an incident, the reporting officer records one weapon/force used type for shotgun. In addition, offense records with multiple weapon/force involved types are counted more than once in the table.

Table	Data Used	Construction
9	NIBRS Offense Segment	This table shows the number of offense records reporting the use of alcohol, computer equipment, and/or drugs by <u>any</u> of the offenders. As offenders may have used more than one type in an offense, the table does not reflect a count of offenders.
10	NIBRS Arrestee Segment	Numbers in the table count the number of arrestees based on the UCR Arrest Offense Code found in the arrestee segment. Each arrestee is counted only once in the table.
11	NIBRS Arrestee Segment	Arrestee ages were collapsed into groups. The table numbers equal the total number of arrestees reported. Each arrestee is counted only once in the table.
12	NIBRS Arrestee Segment	The table numbers equal the total number of arrestees as reported by gender. Each arrestee is counted only once in the table.
13	NIBRS Arrestee Segment	The table numbers equal the total number of arrestees as reported by race. Each arrestee is counted only once in the table.
14	NIBRS Arrestee Segment	The table numbers equal the total number of arrestees as reported by ethnicity. Each arrestee is counted only once in the table. Arrestee ethnicity is an optional NIBRS field.
15	NIBRS Arrestee Segment	The table numbers equal the total number of arrestees as reported by resident status. Each arrestee is counted only once in the table. Arrestee resident status is an optional NIBRS field.
A	NIBRS Offense and Victim Segments	The table counts the number of offenses for each offense type by year. Crimes against persons count one offense for each victim which is determined by the victim segment *Victim Connected to UCR Offense Code(s)* data element and can link up to 10 offense codes to the victim. Both crimes against property and society count only one offense per distinct operation which is determined by the offense segment.
B	NIBRS Offense Segment	This table has a unique unit of count. It is the number of weapon types found in offense records. Therefore, the table can be read as "there were 86,312 personal weapon types associated with simple assault offense records." However, it can also be read as "there were 86,312 simple assault records associated with personal weapons." This table does not count one offense for each victim of crimes against persons and only includes offense types for which weapon type is collected.

Appendix E: NIBRS Segments, Data Elements, and Their Use in This Study

56 NIBRS Data Elements	Data Elements used in this study

ADMINISTRATIVE

1   Originating Agency Identifier (ORI) Number
2   Incident Number
3   Incident Date/Hour ⟶ Table 2, Table 7, Appendix A
4   Cleared Exceptionally
5   Exceptional Clearance Date

OFFENSE

6   UCR Offense Code ⟶ Table 2 - Number of Offense Records, Appendices A & B
7   Offense Attempted/Completed
8   Offender(s) Suspected of Using ⟶ Table 9
8A Bias Motivation
9   Location Type ⟶ Code 22, School/College (includes universities)
10 Number of Premises Entered
11 Method of Entry
12 Type Criminal Activity/Gang Information
13 Type Weapon/Force Involved ⟶ Table 8, Appendix B

PROPERTY

14 Type Property Loss/Etc.
15 Property Description
16 Value of Property
17 Date Recovered
18 Number of Stolen Motor Vehicles
19 Number of Recovered Motor Vehicles
20 Suspected Drug Type
21 Estimated Drug Quantity
22 Type Drug Measurement

VICTIM

23   Victim (Sequence) Number
24   Victim Connected to UCR Offense Code(s)
25   Type of Victim
25A Type of Activity (Officer)/Circumstance
25B Assignment Type (Officer)
25C ORI—Other Jurisdiction (Officer)
26   Age (of Victim)
27   Sex (of Victim)
28   Race (of Victim)
29   Ethnicity (of Victim)
30   Resident Status (of Victim)
31   Aggravated Assault/Homicide Circumstances
32   Additional Justifiable Homicide Circumstances
33   Type Injury
34   Offender Number(s) to be Related
35   Relationship(s) of Victim to Offender(s) ⟶ Table 6

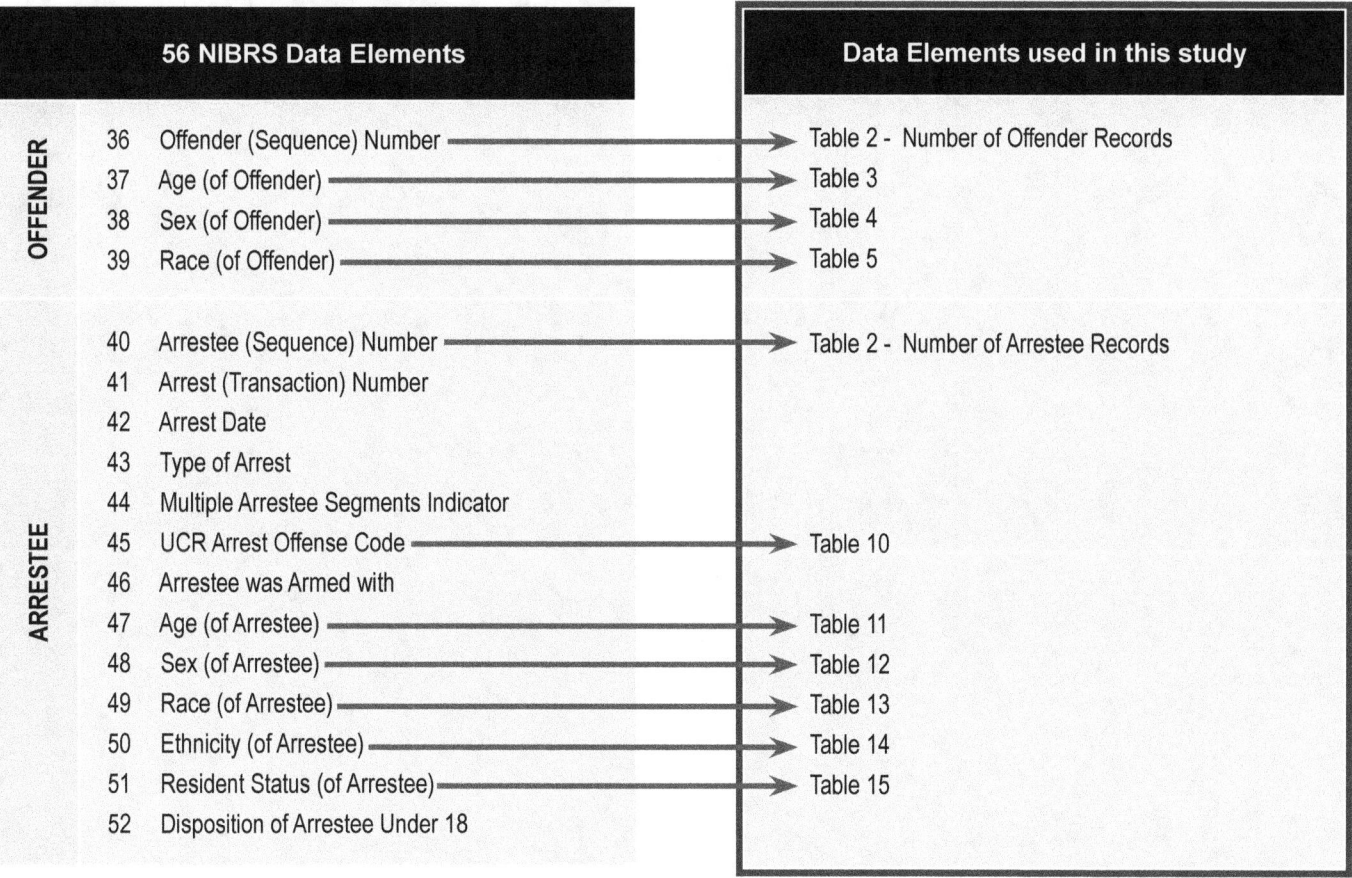

56 NIBRS Data Elements	Data Elements used in this study

OFFENDER

36 Offender (Sequence) Number → Table 2 - Number of Offender Records
37 Age (of Offender) → Table 3
38 Sex (of Offender) → Table 4
39 Race (of Offender) → Table 5

ARRESTEE

40 Arrestee (Sequence) Number → Table 2 - Number of Arrestee Records
41 Arrest (Transaction) Number
42 Arrest Date
43 Type of Arrest
44 Multiple Arrestee Segments Indicator
45 UCR Arrest Offense Code → Table 10
46 Arrestee was Armed with
47 Age (of Arrestee) → Table 11
48 Sex (of Arrestee) → Table 12
49 Race (of Arrestee) → Table 13
50 Ethnicity (of Arrestee) → Table 14
51 Resident Status (of Arrestee) → Table 15
52 Disposition of Arrestee Under 18